INSECTS

Published by Creative Education, Inc., 123 South Broad Street, Mankato, Minnesota 56001

Printed by permission of Wildlife Education, Ltd.

ISBN 0-88682-335-8

INSECTS

Created and Written by
John Bonnett Wexo

Zoological Consultant
Charles R. Schroeder, D.V.M.
Director Emeritus
San Diego Zoo &
San Diego Wild Animal Park

Scientific Consultants
Thomas Eisner, Ph.D.
Schurmann Professor of Biology
Cornell University

Edward J. Maruska
Director
Cincinnati Zoological Gardens

Ronald E. Monroe, Ph.D.
Department of Zoology
San Diego State University

Creative Education

Art Credits

All paintings by Walter Stuart, with assistance from Sfona Pelah.

Photographic Credits

Front Cover: Darwin Dale *(Photo Researchers);* **Pages Six and Seven:** John Gerlach *(Tom Stack & Associates);* **Page Eight: Top,** Kjell B. Sandved; **Left** L. West *(Bruce Coleman, Inc.);* **Right,** Tom McHugh *(Photo Researchers);* **Page Nine: Top Left,** Stephen Dalton *(Photo Researchers);* **Top Right,** Andy Crosthwaite *(Earth Images);* **Bottom Left,** H. Uible *(Photo Researchers);* **Bottom Right,** Peter Ward *(Bruce Coleman, Inc.);* **Page Ten:** John Shaw *(Tom Stack & Associates);* **Page Eleven:** Kiell B. Sandved; **Page Twelve: Top Right, Middle Right, and Bottom Right,** Kjell B. Sandved; **Left,** Hans Pfietschinger *(Peter Arnold, Inc.);* **Page Thirteen: Top Left,** Michael Fogden *(Bruce Coleman, Inc.);* **Top Right,** C. Allan Morgan *(Peter Arnold, Inc.);* **Bottom Left,** Stephen Dalton *(Photo Researchers);* **Bottom Right,** Kjell B. Sandved; **Page Fourteen: Top Left,** John H. Gerard *(Bruce Coleman, Inc.);* **Top Middle,** Kjell B. Sandved; **Top Right,** John H. Gerard *(Bruce Coleman, Inc.):* **Second Row, Left,** Gwen Fidler *(Tom Stack & Associates);* **Middle,** John Shaw *(Tom Stack & Associates);* **Right,** John H. Gerard *(Bruce Coleman, Inc.);* **Third Row, Left,** Kjell B. Sandved; **Middle,** E. R. Degginger *(Bruce Coleman, Inc.);* **Right,** Kjell B. Sandved; **Bottom Left,** Gwen Fidler *(Tom Stack & Associates);* **Page Fifteen: Top Left,** Stephen Dalton *(Photo Researchers).*

Middle Left, Rod Planck *(Tom Stack & Associates);* **Bottom Left,** Kjell B. Sandved; **Middle,** Michael Ederegger *(Peter Arnold, Inc.);* **Top Right,** Runk/Schoenberger *(Grant Heilman);* **Middle Right,** Kim Taylor *(Bruce Coleman, Ltd.);* **Bottom Right,** John Shaw *(Tom Stack & Associates);* **Page Sixteen: Top,** Mik Dakin *(Bruce Coleman, Ltd.);* **Left,** N. Smythe *(Photo Researchers);* **Right,** Dr. Crich *(Okapia);* **Page Seventeen:** Carol Hughes *(Bruce Coleman, Inc.);* **Page Eighteen: Top Left,** John Gerard *(DRK Photos);* **Bottom Right, Bottom Left, Middle Left, and Top Right,** Kjell B. Sandved; **Page Nineteen: Top Left,** F. Glenn Erwin *(Cyr Color Photo Agency);* **Top and Middle Right, Middle, Bottom Left and Right,** Kjell B. Sandved; **Pages Twenty and Twenty-one:** Kjell B. Sandved; **Page Twenty-two: Top Right,** Kjell B. Sandved; **Top Left,** Doug Wechsler; **Middle,** Ian Beames *(Ardea London);* **Bottom Left and Middle,** Becky & Gary Vestal *(Earth Images);* Bottom Right, Kjell B. Sandved; Page Twenty-three: Top Right and **Left, MiddleRight and Left,** Kjell B. Sandved; **Bottom Right,** Hans Pfietschinger *(Peter Arnold, Inc.);* **Bottom Left,** P.H. Ward *(Natural Science Photos).*

Our Thanks To: Amadeo Rea and David Faulkner *(San Diego Museum of Natural History);* Ernie Chew; Bill Knerr and Bob Ward *(San Diego Zoological Society);* Bonnie Sumner; Alletat McDonald *(San Diego Flora society);* Lynnette Wexo.

Creative Education would like to thank Wildlife Education, Ltd., for granting them the rights to print and distribute this hardbound edition.

Contents

Insects have a bad reputation. We tend to think of them as unpleasant little pests that bite or sting. Some damage our trees and plants, and a few carry diseases. But when we take a closer look, we discover a fascinating and beautiful world on a miniature scale. And we also begin to realize how important insects are.

In fact, insects as a group are often far more beneficial to nature than people think. They help plants and trees to grow. They provide food for birds and other animals. And they help to make the world a cleaner place to live.

Insects are also important because they are everywhere. Three-fourths of all animals alive are insects. There may be as many as 200,000 for every human being. One reason people may dislike insects is that there are so many of them. And we can't seem to control them. In fact, insects are the only group of animals that don't seem to be bothered by things people do. Often, the more we try to destroy them, the more they seem to thrive.

Compared to people, all insects are small. But in some ways, smaller can be better. It allows insects to live successfully in more different kinds of places than any other group of animals. They abound in plants and trees. They live under nearly every rock. They thrive on the surface of the ground and under the ground. Many live beside ponds and streams, some live on the water, and a few even live under water.

While many animals have become extinct because they failed to adapt to changes in their environment, insects seem able to adapt to almost anything. They were among the first animals to climb out of the water and live on land. They were the very first to develop wings and take to the air. Some of them can live in very cold places, and others can live in very hot places.

Part of the reason that insects have been so successful is their tremendous variety. Even though all insects have the same basic body parts, they have been developed in thousands of different ways to take advantage of every possible form of food and every possible habitat. This has led to a marvelous array of colors and shapes in the insect world. As with most animals, the more you learn about insects, the more you appreciate them. Who knows, you may even be more careful where you step!

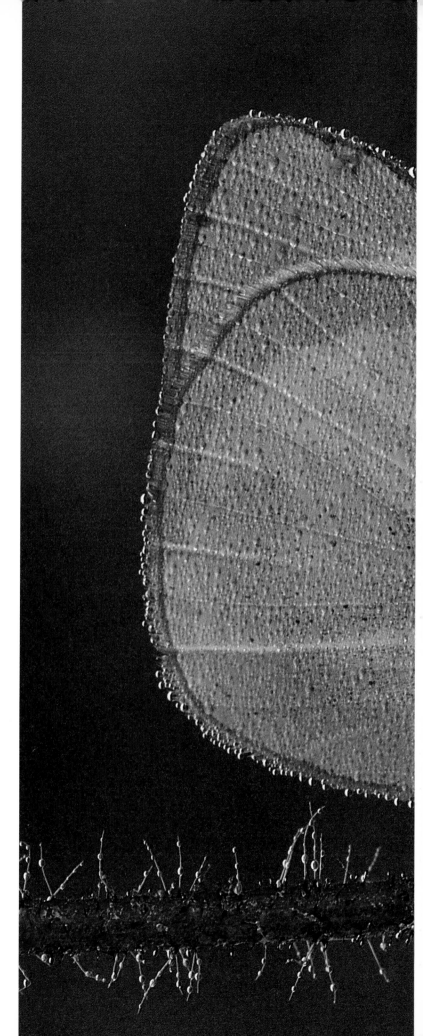

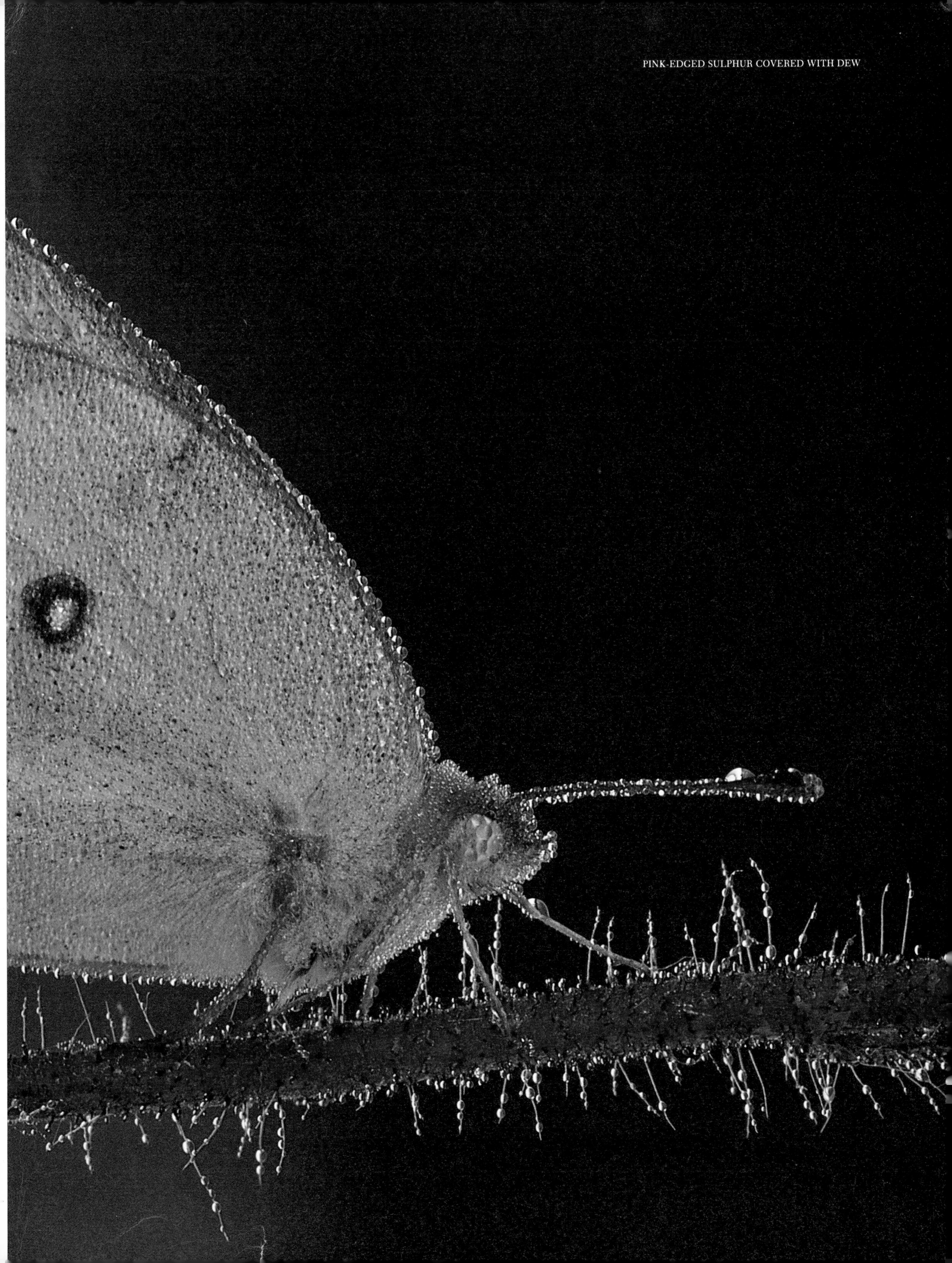

PINK-EDGED SULPHUR COVERED WITH DEW

What is an insect? Many people think all tiny animals that crawl are insects. They think spiders, scorpions, mites, centipedes, millipedes, crabs, and even lobsters are insects. But none of these animals is an insect. They may *look* like insects, but once you know what to look for, you will see that they are not.

One difference between insects and all other animals is the number of legs they have. In the entire animal kingdom, only insects have six legs. Another thing you can look for is the number of wings. Most adult insects have 4 wings, and no other animals do. Also, insects have *two antennae* (AN-TEN-EYE) on their heads. These sense organs are usually located right between the eyes.

On these pages, there is only one true insect. Can you find it without reading the captions on the pictures? If you can't, don't worry. This book will help you learn how to tell the difference between insects and other animals.

MILLIPEDE

Can this be an insect? It is called a *millipede* (MILL-uh-peed), which means "thousand legged." Millipedes don't actually have a thousand legs, but they have too many legs to be insects.

VELVET MITE

This little animal certainly looks like an insect. But if you look closely, you will see that it has no antennae. So it cannot be an insect, because all insects have two antennae on their heads.

THAI CENTIPEDE

GRASSHOPPER

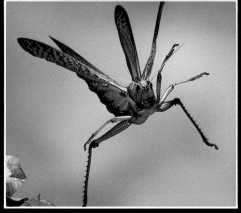

Count the number of legs on this animal. Count its wings and its antennae. You are right—this grasshopper is an insect! It has six legs, four wings, and two antennae.

GIANT WOOD LOUSE

This little animal has many names. It is called a "sowbug," a "pillbug," and a "woodlouse." It has antennae like insects do. But it isn't an insect, because it has *too many* antennae—and too many legs.

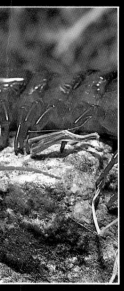

This creature has two large antennae—but it isn't an insect. It's a *centipede* (CENT-uh-peed), which means "hundred-legged." It is closely related to the millipede, as you may have guessed. Like the millipede, it has too many legs to be an insect.

People often think that spiders are insects. And at first glance, they look like insects. But they are not very closely related. For one thing, spiders have eight legs instead of six. And they don't have wings or antennae.

WOLF SPIDER

YELLOW SAHARAN SCORPION

Scorpions are close relatives of spiders. They have long, slender bodies like insects. But scorpions don't have wings or antennae. So they cannot be insects.

The body of an insect is a masterpiece of design. In many ways, insect bodies are much more efficient than our own. The basic design is quite simple. The bodies of all insects are divided into three sections, as shown at right. The sections common to all insects are the *head*, the *thorax* (THORE-ax), and the *abdomen* (AB-doe-mun).

The head has two eyes, two antennae, and a mouth. Insects eat a wide variety of food. And to do this, they have a wide variety of mouth shapes. But there are really only four basic kinds of mouths. Some insects have mouths that *soak up* liquids like sponges. Others have mouths that are made for *sucking*. Many have mouths that *pierce* like hypodermic needles. And a large number of them use their mouths for *crushing and chewing*.

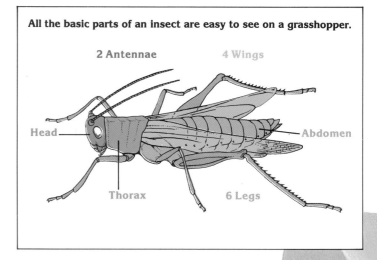

All the basic parts of an insect are easy to see on a grasshopper.

2 Antennae   4 Wings

Head

Abdomen

Thorax   6 Legs

Flies belong to a group of insects called *diptera* (DIP-turr-uh), which means "two wings." But don't let the name fool you. They really have four wings like other insects. However, the back two are just tiny stubs that are usually hidden beneath the front wings. See if you can find the back two "wings" on this fly.

This fly has long mouth parts that end in a broad tip. The tip is porous, and the fly uses it like a sponge to soak up water and other liquids. Can you find the fly's sponging mouth parts?

GREEN BOTTLE FLY

MOSQUITO ON HUMAN ARM

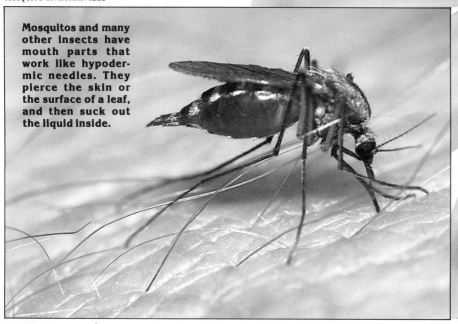

Mosquitos and many other insects have mouth parts that work like hypodermic needles. They pierce the skin or the surface of a leaf, and then suck out the liquid inside.

Many insects have mouths that work like ours—they bite and chew. But insects don't have teeth. So they need jaws that are strong and have sharp edges to cut and chew their food. Tiger beetles move their jaws sideways to chew their food, not up and down.

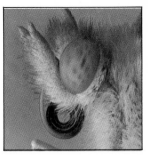

When moths and butterflies aren't using their mouth parts, they can *roll them up* like a hose! The mouths of some moths are actually twice as long as the rest of their bodies.

CHECKERSPOT BUTTERFLY

Moths and butterflies have long mouth parts that look like hoses. They use them to suck nectar from flowers, just like you would sip a milkshake through a straw. Do you see this butterfly's mouth parts sucking nectar from the center of the flower?

TIGER BEETLE

Your skeleton is on the inside of your body. But insects have theirs on the outside. This kind of skeleton is called an *exoskeleton* (EX-oh-skel-uh-ton). It supports the muscles inside the insect's body. And it gives the little insect a "coat of armor" for protection.

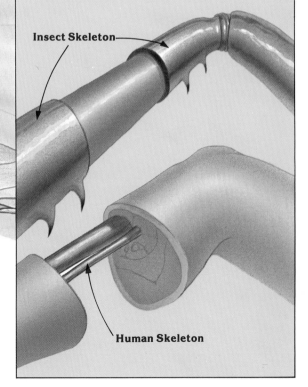

Insect Skeleton

Human Skeleton

A spectacular variety of shapes has developed out of the basic insect design. All three sections of the body can grow into very strange forms. In general, the weird bodies of insects help them to survive in one way or another.

The bodies of many insects are made for hiding. Some hide and wait to ambush their prey. Others hide to keep predators from finding them. An insect may escape from predators because it looks like part of a tree, plant, or flower.

Some insects want to be seen. Their bodies may look scary to keep predators away. Others have "horns" that can be used for fighting with other insects. Some have stingers they can use for defense or for killing their prey. And many insects have hard "shells" that protect them like armor.

This beetle uses its exoskeleton like a turtle uses its shell. If it is attacked, it simply hides under its "shell." It has large feet that can grip leaves or stems with incredible strength. When predators can't pull the beetle over, they give up and go away.

TORTOISE BEETLE

NORTH AMERICAN TREEHOPPER

The prize for "weirdest-looking insects" goes to the treehoppers. They all have odd formations on their backs. The one shown above looks like a thorn. The one below looks like it came from another planet. Scientists are not sure why it is shaped this way.

This insect looks like it's made of dead leaves and sticks. This makes it hard to see when it hides among real leaves and sticks—so predators are less likely to find it.

LARVA OF AUSTRALIAN WALKING STICK

SOUTH AMERICAN TREEHOPPER

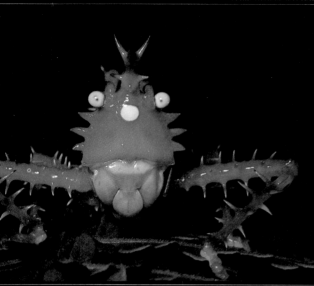

Walking sticks like to "hang around" in some pretty odd positions. By doing this, they can make themselves look like twigs. And very often, predators don't even see them.

Even the most fearsome predator would think twice before attacking this katydid. The sharp spikes covering its body look dangerous. But the katydid is harmless and does not attack other insects.

The beetle with the longer "horns" will probably win this battle. The horns of the male Stag beetle are really just huge jaws. Their only purpose seems to be for fighting other males, usually over a female.

A wasp can aim its stinger in any direction. This is because the abdomen is separated from the thorax by a flexible rod called a *petiole* (PET-ee-ol). The Mud Dauber wasp has an unusually long petiole. See if you can find it.

The way insects grow seems strange and magical. It is called *metamorphosis* (MET-UH-MORE-FUH-SIS), which means "a change of form." Most insects go through 4 separate stages in metamorphosis. They start as an *egg*, become a *larva* (LAR-VUH), then a *pupa* (PYU-PUH), and finally an *adult*.

The larva that hatches from the egg is very different from the adult. It has no wings and often eats different foods than the adult. As a pupa, the growing insect eats nothing at all. It seems to be doing nothing. But it is quietly changing into an adult. The stages of metamorphosis for a Monarch butterfly are shown below.

This adult butterfly has completed its metamorphosis. It is ready to fly away and find a mate.

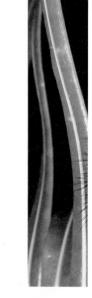

1 The egg of the Monarch butterfly looks like a precious gem. A female butterfly may produce hundreds of eggs in one summer. It takes four or five days for each one to hatch.

2 When it first hatches, the caterpillar is tiny. But it grows so quickly that it must replace its "skin" every few days to make room for a bigger body. In two weeks, it grows 2,700 times its original size!

3 After two weeks, the caterpillar spins a silk "button" to attach itself upside down to a leaf or branch.

4 Next, the larva replaces its skin with a tough pupa case. The pupa of a butterfly is often called a *chrysalis* (CHRIS-ul-us).

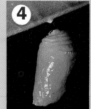

5 Within a few days, the pupa begins to look like an adult. Its bright orange-and-black wings begin to take shape.

6 Two weeks after the chrysalis is formed, the adult breaks the case and climbs out, head first.

IO MOTH CATERPILLAR

TUSSOCK MOTH CATERPILLAR

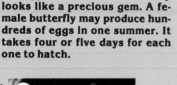
SPICEBUSH SWALLOWTAIL CATERPILLAR

Caterpillars are the larvae of moths and butterflies. They have a wonderful variety of shapes. And many of them are very colorful.

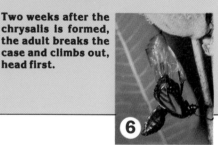
HICKORY HORN DEVIL

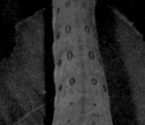

Many common insects do not go through all four stages of metamorphosis. Grasshoppers, crickets, dragonflies, and many others do not have a pupa stage. Their larvae look like wingless adults. One of the most fascinating of these is the Periodical *cicada* (suh-KAY-duh). Its larvae live underground for *17 years* before they emerge as adults!

ADULT PERIODICAL CICADA

At first, its wings are too small and soft for flying. Usually the adult emerges on a bright sunny day, so it only takes about two hours for its wings to expand and dry.

ADULT MOSQUITO

The larvae of mosquitos live in a completely different environment than the adults. They hang upside down under the surface of a pond or stream, as shown below. They breathe through tiny tubes. After their pupa stage, the adults rise from the water as shown at right. Then they fly away to live on land.

TIGER MOTH CATERPILLAR

The shapes and colors of caterpillars may help protect them from predators in different ways. Some colorful patterns look scary. The sharp spikes and fuzzy hairs on other caterpillars make them hard to swallow.

MOSQUITO LARVAE

15

Insects can move with astonishing speed and agility. For their size, they can run faster, climb higher, jump farther, or fly more swiftly than most other animals.

Very few insects can do all of these things with equal skill. Some have good wings for flying from plant to plant, or for catching prey, or for escaping from predators. Others are not such good fliers, but they may be extremely fast runners, or excellent climbers. Many insects that live on small bushes are superb jumpers. And most insects that live in the water are great divers and swimmers.

HOVER FLY

A helicopter looks clumsy next to a Hover fly. This small insect can hover in one place for hours. And it can land in any position you can think of.

IO MOTH

GRASSHOPPER

Grasshoppers can jump more than 40 times the length of their own bodies. If people could jump that well, a man could leap 240 feet (73 meters) in a single bound. The back legs of grasshoppers have very large muscles to provide power for jumping. The muscles store energy like the springs on pogo sticks, so they can shoot the grasshoppers up into the air.

GREAT DIVING BEETLE

16

Insect muscles never get tired, like human muscles do. If an insect could eat enough food, it could keep running or flying for days! People can't do this because they can't supply oxygen to their muscles fast enough. Without oxygen, the muscles get tired. But insects can breathe oxygen directly through many tiny holes, called *spiracles* (SPEAR-uh-kulls), located along the sides of their bodies. They can supply more oxygen to their muscles, and so the muscles don't get tired.

How would you like to climb to the top of Mt. Everest every day, and then climb down again carrying somebody on your back? Leafcutter ants are only a fraction of an inch long, but every day they climb 200-foot trees (61 meters). For their size, that's the same as climbing Mt. Everest. Then they carry down pieces of leaf that weigh as much as they do.

Moths have to be very acrobatic fliers to get away from bats that prey on them. They can change direction with a speed and agility that human fliers can only dream about. A moth can make hundreds of turns in less than a minute.

LEAFCUTTER ANT

Diving beetles take air with them when they dive, just like human scuba divers. But the beetles can do something with the air that no human diver can do. They can use the bubble on their backs to draw extra oxygen directly out of the water.

layers of exoskeleton. These are held together by thin, hollow rods, called *veins*.

The veins make the wings very strong. Some butterflies can fly thousands of miles on wings that are thinner than a piece of paper. As you will see on these pages, insects use their wings in different ways.

LUNA MOTH

Some moths have wings so thin that you can almost see through them. A few, like this Luna moth, have clear spots on their wings that you actually *can* see through.

Scientists call moths and butterflies *lepidoptera* (lep-uh-DOP-turr-uh). The name means "scaled wings." It fits this group of insects because their wings are covered with thousands of tiny scales. That's what gives many moths and butterflies their wonderful colors.

SATURNID MOTH

Notice how the wings of this beautiful moth overlap. They fit this way so that the front and back wings can move together as one big wing. With so much wing area, butterflies and moths do not have to flap their wings as fast as insects with smaller wings.

Most insects can fold their wings when they are not using them. But some cannot, like this Damsel fly. Its wings are of a primitive design. The wings of the earliest flying insects may have looked like this.

You can see thousands of colorful little scales on the wing of this moth. If you could lift the scales with your fingers, you would see the clear, thin wing underneath.

The front wings on a beetle are ha[rd] and thick. They are not used for f[ly]ing. Instead, they protect the ba[ck] wings by covering them when t[he] wings are folded. In order to fly, t[he] beetle raises its front wings a[nd] releases the back ones.

SCARAB BEE[TLE]

LONG-LEGGED FLY

Insects with small wings may move them very fast. This fly can beat its wings 200 times per second. Mosquitos flap their wings 600 times a second, and tiny midges can move their wings up and down *1,000 times every second!*

DAMSEL FLY

VEINS OF GRASSHOPPER WING

GRASSHOPPER

Some insects do not have to flap their wings all the time to stay in the air. When grasshoppers jump, they unfold their back wings and let the wind carry them along. Of course, they don't always glide like this. They can also flap their wings, and sometimes fly great distances.

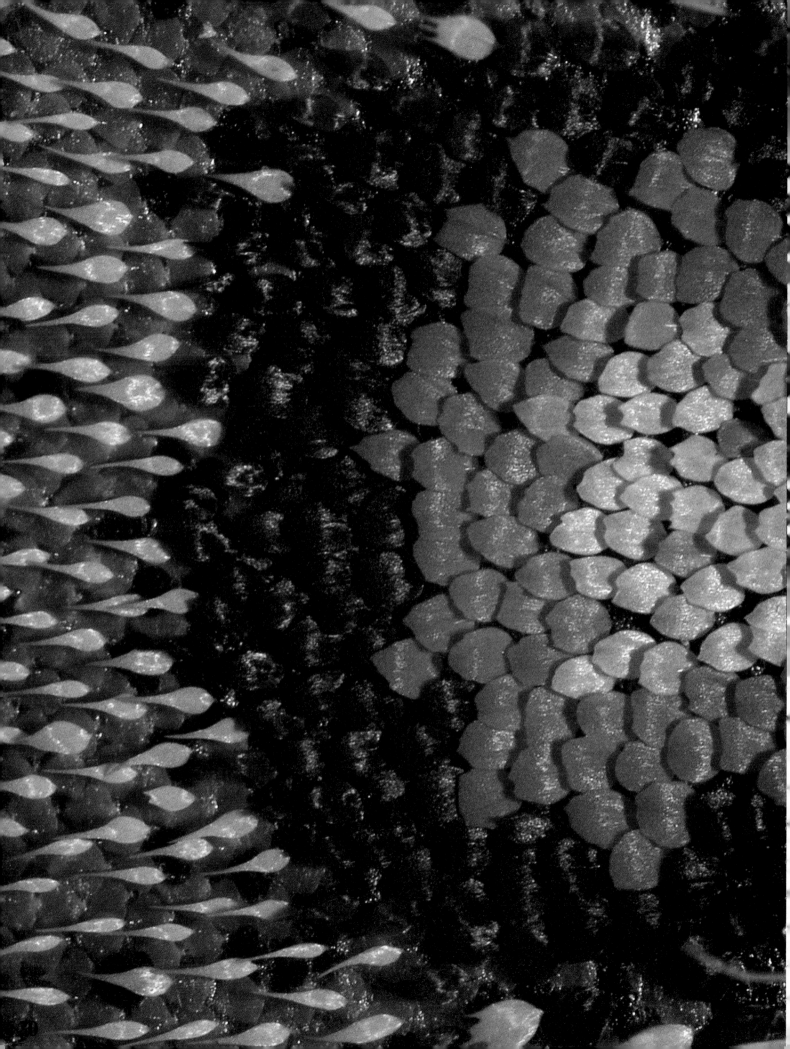

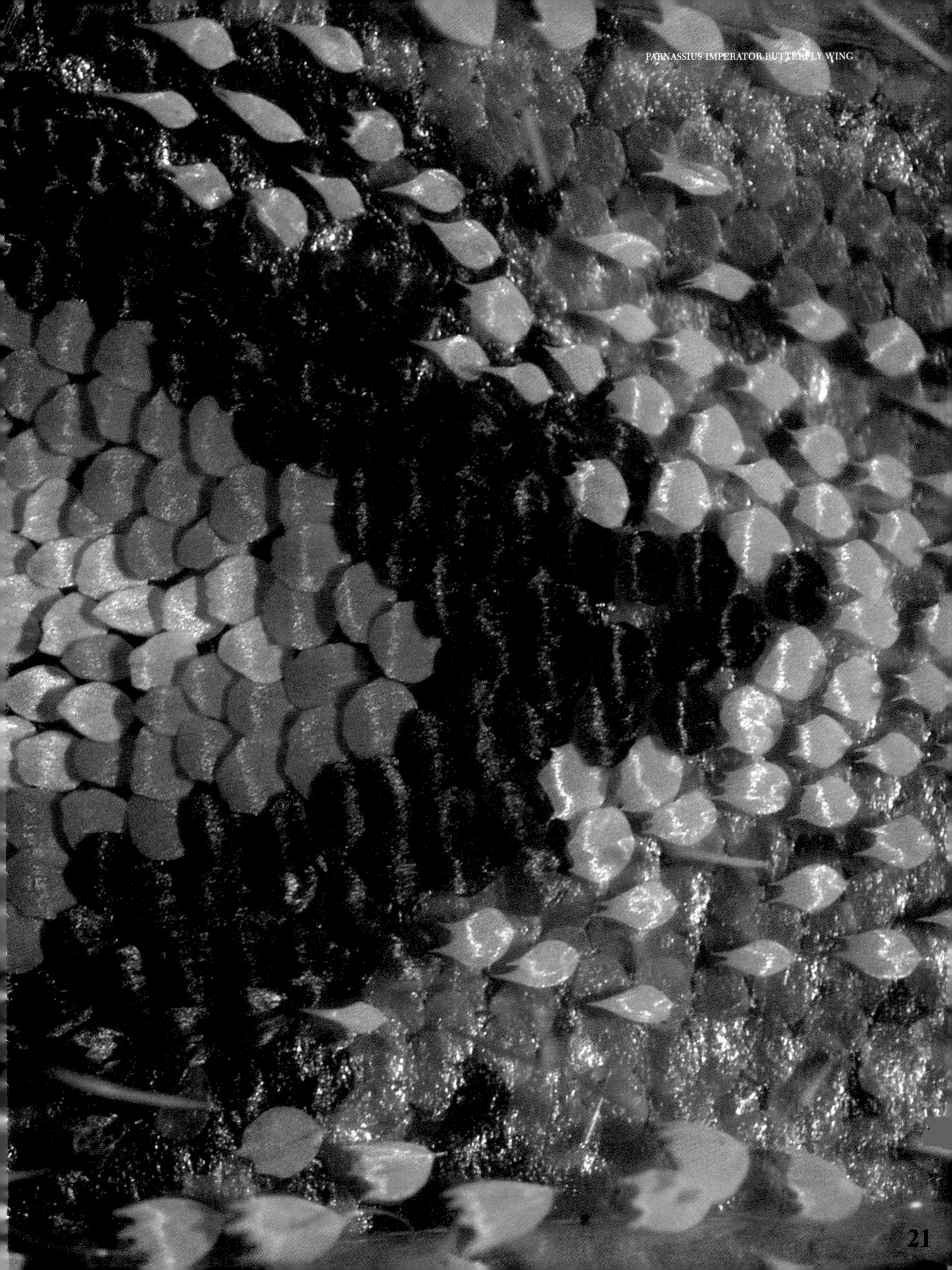

Color is found everywhere in the world of insects. Many insects look incredibly beautiful to us. But the insects themselves don't care about beauty. To them, color may be a matter of survival.

Insects use color to keep themselves alive in 3 different ways. First, they may use it to *camouflage* themselves, making it harder for other insects to see them. Second, some insects use *bright colors* as a warning to predators. The colors tell predators that these insects may be poisonous or bad tasting. Third, some insects may *imitate* the bright colors of other insects to make predators *think* they are bad to eat. These insects aren't really poisonous or bad tasting, but they fool predators into thinking they are.

This moth's brilliant colors are a warning that it has a *terrible taste*. It also has a tiny "face" on its back. But nobody is really sure if this also helps protect it. Can you find the face on the moth's back?

TIGER MOTH

BARK MANTIS

LANTERN FLY

Some insects have markings that defend them in more than one way. For example, the Lantern fly shown above has an effective camouflage. But it also has markings that can confuse predators. It has real eyes on one end of its body, and false eyes on the other end. A predator that sees it may have trouble telling which way the Lantern fly is going.

Now you see it—now you don't! This mantis is so well camouflaged that it seems to disappear before your very eyes.

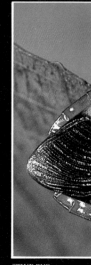

STINK BUG

BLINDED SPHINX MOTH

BLINDED SPHINX MOTH

Many moths also have double protection. First, their front wings may be used to camouflage them. When these wings are folded back, the moth may be hard to see Ⓐ. Second, their rear wings may have bright "eyespots" to frighten predators away. To flash its eyespots, a moth simply spreads its front wings Ⓑ. The sudden appearance of the "eyes" startles a bird or other predator, so the moth can fly away unharmed.

The amazing color patterns on this beetle are really a sign that says, "Poison—Don't Eat Me!" One bite is enough to make many predators sick.

This katydid keeps its color hidden until it is needed. When it senses danger, the katydid stands on its head like an acrobat. This reveals markings on the underside of its body that make it look like a wasp.

LEAF BEETLE

LEAF BEETLE

The patterns on these beetles look as if an artist painted them with a paintbrush. In a sense, they *are* painted on, because they are caused by pigments— the same kinds of chemicals that make color in paint.

The bright colors on this bug tell predators that it has a *terrible smell*. When attackers come too close, it sprays a foul smelling chemical into the air.

HORNET MOTH

HOVER FLY

Some insects are "actors." They have "costumes" that fool predators. These insects are usually harmless. They have no sting, no poison, not even a bad taste. But their costumes may be enough to keep predators from eating them. For example, the fly on the left looks like a honey bee. And the moth at right is imitating a wasp.

Index